Playful Song Called Beautiful

Playful Song Called Beautiful

POEMS BY

JOHN BLAIR

UNIVERSITY OF IOWA PRESS | *Iowa City*

University of Iowa Press, Iowa City 52242
Copyright © 2016 by John Blair
www.uiowapress.org
Printed in the United States of America

Design by Kathleen Szawiola

The University of Iowa Press is a member of Green Press Initiative and is committed to preserving natural resources.

Printed on acid-free paper

Library of Congress Cataloging-in-Publication Data
Names: Blair, John, 1961– author.
Title: Playful song called beautiful / John Blair.
Description: Iowa City: University of Iowa Press, [2016] |
    Series: Iowa Poetry Prize
Identifiers: LCCN 2015035316 | ISBN 978-1-60938-399-2 (pbk) |
    ISBN 978-1-60938-400-5 (ebk)
Classification: LCC PS3602.L335 A6 2016 | DDC 811/.6—dc23
LC record available at http://lccn.loc.gov/2015035316

Cover art and art on pages ii–iii by Sandra Hoekman-Blair

I have spent whole days scribbling down nonsense.
YOSHIDA KENKO, *Essays in Idleness*

Contents

⁓

Acknowledgments   ix

How to Know Two   1
Dirt   2
To a Girl Walking Away From the British Museum   5
The Idle Hours   7
Blue Moon   10
The Horse   14
A Philosophy of Gravity   15
Disagreeable Things   17
The One Thing   19
What Happens to the Future   22
The Truth You Heard   25
Sleeping Dogs Lie   26
Goethe's Apple   28
Three Quarks for Muster Mark   32
A Song on Geronimo's Grave   37
The Law of the Excluded Middle   43
Hard Pearl   45

The Lesser Poet   46

And Yet It Moves   48

Playful Song Called Beautiful   50

The Lost Children   51

The Thing Itself Speaks   53

What We Want   56

Quod Me Nutrit Me Destruit   58

Evil Pockets   64

Desirada   69

The Ghosts of Birds   71

Why You Leave   72

If I Should Die Before I Wake   73

The Gift   74

What Happens When You Stop   76

What is Left   77

Dog Dreams   78

Mésalliance Grotesque   79

Turing Lies with Men   81

Blood Rain at Stoke Edith   83

Here Where We Are Terrible   86

The Things You Can't Keep   90

Shooting Dove   94

Acknowledgments

~

Poems in this collection have been published in the following journals and magazines:

"Disagreeable Things," *Café Review*; "The Thing Itself Speaks," *Carolina Quarterly*; "The Ghosts of Birds," *Denver Quarterly*; "Dirt," *The Florida Review*; "The Lesser Poet," *The Florida Review*; "And Yet It Moves," *The Florida Review*; "Sleeping Dogs Lie," *Iron Horse Literary Review*; "The Things You Can't Keep," *Nimrod*; "Blood Rain at Stoke Edith," *Poetry Quarterly*; "The Idle Hours," *Ruminate*; "The Truth You Heard," *Ruminate*; "The One Thing," *Ruminate*; "Hard Pearl," *Ruminate*; "What Happens to the Future," *Solstice*; "How to Know Two," *The Southern Review*; "Blue Moon," *Spoon River Poetry Review*; "Desirada," *Tar River Poetry Review*; "Playful Song Called Beautiful," *Thema*

Playful Song Called Beautiful

How to Know Two

⌒

We used to think that if we knew one, we knew two, because one and one
are two. We are finding that we must learn a great deal more about 'and.'
—SIR ARTHUR STANLEY EDDINGTON

Look around, brother;
there is no stranger who is
stranger than you, no

familiar who's more
familiar. The cup's the hole
as much as the clay,

the held as much as
the holding. Your hands, they hum
like a spear of grass

teeth-buzzing against
your sweet contingency, tone
against silence, hard

against tone, hymn-sung
and holy in the split-tongue
garden of our blue

undecideds.
Wherever there is sky there
is something rising,

something falling. That's
all the comfort you need, all
the comfort you get.

Dirt

〜

Has stages like grief,
from *it breaks you or you break*
it to *it breaks you*

anyway. Dirt is
process. Dirt is shit and sweat
and hard clay lessons.

Come spring, your father
planted gardens that were fields
of ambition, half-

acre works of *son*
of a bitch and blisters packed
tight as pinfeathers

on your hands fresh from
the hopeful breasts of the girl
with leukemia

from up the road who
played you pale cards and checkers
on Sundays and asked

you without looking
at you into the cabin
of her daddy's boat

high-trailered under
a half-magnolia fat-leaved
and lopsided where

the linesmen had chain-
sawed one side away to clear
the surging power

lines. No secret so
deep-dirt kept and shameless,
turned under the mud-

furrowed sloughs of by-
gone and damned-near forgotten.
So little survives,

besides the gall stained
stubbornness of things and all
the holes and gutters

we shove them into.
Dirt skins the world like curd, like
slick palm-sweat, or grease

white-icing cold dish
water in a boat galley
sink where you alone

sit crying in fish
stink darkness for the sweetness
that is a loss not

really your own, sweet
because it's only the shade
of pain and not its

rusty teeth, grief you
can stuff unmourned into a
tiny doll-grave dug

into a half-acre
of cold clay loam, a *shabti*
of blue glazed faience

scratched with careful runes
from the *Book of the Dead* which
read *let everything*

which stands in the way
be removed; whether to plough
fields, or soak the dirt

or carry sand from
East to West, "Here am I," you
shall say, "for only

you shall I do it."

To a Girl Walking Away from the British Museum

⁓

All those alder leaves sifting bright fisheyes
across the pavement's sunspalled back, blown from
Achilles' shield whereon the sightless stream
of Ocean churns gray circle past the dumb

City of Peace, littered with flotsam and
mislaid children slow-rolled in Ocean's cheeks.
A callow girl walks Briseis-eyed between
the black-wrought gates onto Great William Street,

disconsolate with knowing, with surfeits
of *old*. Though she is not a daughter of
Lycomedes, not the jaded one who is
forever leaving in cool bas-relief

as keen Odysseus sunders cross-dressed
Achilles from his flower-print *peplos*,
she does not doubt herself, does not linger
among the sisters-who-fawn, cold-chiseled

on some sarcophagus. She is never
the marble or its meaning, not a girl
engraved upon a box, but the cool space
inside where evening glisters and pearls

onto the pagan streets awash with pools
of possibility, where she in pure
ennui appears around the day's contrite
corners, to ripple feral and demure

inside an *adytum* of alder trees,
resigned beneath the changed apparent mind
of some gray moon to just one life spent wild
in any world she leaves unloved behind.

The Idle Hours

~

I have spent whole days scribbling down nonsense.

—YOSHIDA KENKO, *Essays in Idleness*

Every day we fill.
Every day lucky stars and skin
grate into tender

praise and tarry ash,
and eight cylinders of flesh
buckle in and clench

like a fist. Kenko
before his inkstone scribbles
what a strange, insane

feeling this gives me,
every day pearls of grieving,
yellow like pus, like

heart-grease, silting past
his tongue and under his bones.
Every day, he finds

something new he does
not need and shelves it gently
with the thousand things

he does not deserve.
And every day he walks the
random self that falls

from his mouth among
the subdued cattle and swine
and becomes them all,

hoof and hair and fate.
The longer a man lives the
more shame he endures.

In the small wounded
copse of trees beyond the road,
a young housecat stalks

thin streaks of perfect
being through the yellowed grass,
where broken bottles

scalpel every day
into slivers of breath and
purest joy. Soon, her

feral heart will flare
in someone's sobbing headlights,
or in the yellow

mendicant grace of
a coyote's teeth. But in
this moment, in this

one perfect idle
hour, the invert vulval bell
of her ear cups the

windy strum of sky,
the cosseted nothing that
is a kind of pity,

and a kind of love,
lost to the grinding weeds and
snailed vacancies

of every place that
shines her off into the deft
glissando of her

abandonment, gift
to the great wide world that is
ours and never ours.

Blue Moon

~

There's this kid, staring
at sheets on a line, watching
actual white clean

sheets sail-cracking hard
under a steady wind like
god's own DTs, like

miracles and thrills,
and Sunday morning Jesus.
He's like second grade

old, like Elmer's Glue
and round scissors-old, ambushed
by a storm that's news

to him, that's humping
ambergris gray right
at his mother's wash

and the stuttered row
of trailers behind it, and there's
some kind of bliss smeared

on his face, greasy
and rare, like he's thinking come
on, motherfucker,

crack into white flame
and shredded thunder, sunder
the wooden weathered

knuckles of shanty
clothespins and show me the way.
Or maybe he's just

afraid, the way we
all are in the face of not
knowing a damned thing

about the world's piss
and candor; maybe a blue
poker chip lucky

lies in his left hip
pocket and a jinx crosses
his baby blue eyes,

maybe he's holding
his breath against the blue smoke
blown from Mexico

and smelling of burned
sugar cane and cattle shit
and half-minute head

stands at the border.
Maybe he knows why the moon
will rise blue every

night to the trick sound
of dogs howling betrayal
at the smoky grease

of grief turning gray
on its starry spit. The dry
ash cozens his lungs

with brittle promises
and burnt candelilla wax.
The storm is itself,

curdled like his mother's
losses and tossed into fact.
A sheet crescendos

and sheds embarrassed
from the line and he opens
his mouth on something

blue as a bolus
of woad, as a birthday song,
as the Sunday school

bible verse that claims
the blueness of a wound doth
cleanse away evil.

And this is his life,
this boy, bliss-stained and afraid,
all he can ever

want to know shivered
into lines of force that care
not one thing for him

as he turns to run
inside, the first parted coins
of hard rain knuckling

cold across his skull
like the good lessons given
to good boys, and no

end to the graven
words black with grit that litter
every plausible

hope with the regret
he's running into, the ruin
of any life he's

running from, clean sheet
gone gray with rain and the blown
dirt of all his years.

The Horse

~

You think of Nietzsche kneeling down, undone
before the broken horse of his inflamed
mind, think you know his grief, the shallow drone

of his *ausgespielt* heart, how he became
the bleeding horse's sides, became the sun
of its resigned regard. You kneel the same

transfigured way, as if you are the one
who's seen the godless germ of genesis
in every bulb and swollen bloom become

the wailing genius of your penitence.
You fall on bended knee inside a raw
ferment of death and shit and failed pretense,

in empty lots and fields of weedy straw,
where seeds gone punk inside their fallen pods
hum carious with insects that draw

in random runes their softly rotting gods.

A Philosophy of Gravity

~

We only are what we deserve, early
to come and early to go, hem and haw.
The body douses every deep and pearly
confine with coal dust and rot, all its raw

temples enameled with pale adipose.
Dull orphans clutter our heavens like pyres
of hair and minor lives, and in the house
in which your childhood wore itself bald-tire

out your father still drowns in the snakebit
night of his long dying. You stand awake
at midnight, count the pills of old mouse shit
compiled upon the kitchen floor to make

astronomies of negligence. A year
your mother's been dead, blown some other-where
by blunt inertia and blood pressure, here
where we are all forgiven forever

just this once; and maybe there's been this low
susurration of something like weeping
beyond a bedroom wall and maybe no
one here much cares, would rather be sleeping

or somewhere else or deaf as the bottle
fly battering itself against the trash
can's lid, enraged by the smell of fertile
potentials, angry at waste, at the waste

of waste which is just spit in god's unjust
eye, bread cast upon the reviled waters.
And here is where perfection forms in us
its perfect lies: that *back* is an altar

of brick on which the past bleeds itself white,
that *home* is any kind of good reason.
The things we were are a sob of streetlight
through wet glass, a song in any season

to ache like dirt inside your cottoned ears;
you hum it when there's nothing left to say,
you sing the words and silence disappears
and all that's left is the going away.

Disagreeable Things

~

Too much furniture,
too many pens. Too many
monks cribbing nickels,

and sleeping in parks.
Kenko in his idleness
squats in the holy

oleander shade,
hair of dog, penitent cramps,
the art of godly

penury shaking
his bowels. *Too many rocks*
and too many trees

make trite a garden's
olive-green and charming ruse.
No beast, no backs, no

love pitched in any
tent except the worms' warm bog
Kenko, crouched, creates.

Leaves eddy in base
pentimento, repentance blown in,
contrition blown out.

Too many children
in a house, too many words,
and far too many

promises. And so
Kenko goes, or went, whim-blown
and humbled, grieving

for agreeable things:
books in a case, the spare dust
we are in a heap.

The One Thing

⁓

And so here's the thing
they say, as if there could be
just one of any

one thing, one dirt, one air,
one cell, one body, breath in,
breath out. The many

is all, pitiless
as the shark's teeth rattling out
of the Cretaceous

into the glass jar on your
son's bedroom shelf. And so here's
the thing in its limned

self, *the wound*, as sage
Rumi would have it, *by which
the light enters us*:

a child, your child, sobs
inside the cankering worm
of his loathing,

rank as father's milk
in the hair shirt of himself.
This, the *ding an sich*

of alone, of *one-*
ness, burns with multiplicity,
the tangled million

helices of our
herald flesh and fate, father
to son to sorrows.

We pay for sacred
things in the blue geld of blood,
in the simony

of best intentions.
The one thing of which you are
certain: what we are

renders us like lard
every sea changing day.
You want the steady

hum of the completed
universe, intoning *Om*
like the open mouth

of no possible
god. You want dry fields salted
with ruin and hard

winters. You want just
one thing to condense itself
inside your weeping

child like the angel
lingering *contrapposto*
inside a blue fog

of perfect marble,
blessed with the hard penitence
of all god's waiting.

What Happens to the Future

~

There is no future.
It's that simple. New Orleans
humps its sodden past

through every razored
moment as we wander down
Canal Street towards

the winter river running
sick with midwestern flux and sweat.
And the rain that falls

is ever new and to no purpose
under heaven, each cold
drop a wanderer whose

slow birth and grand fall.
never leave the eternal *now*.
The past is no more

real, though it presses
caput mortuum against
the mossy slickness

of our eyes, sweated
from every brick and sinter.
Oswald stood curbed

by his pique just there,
Marxist pamphlets and orphan
pain in either hand,

the cool of Texas
autumn already shambling
through the dimestore wool

of his suit. A few
gray blocks east Faulkner crouched
on a balcony

with a BB gun
in the malice of his youth
and shot at lonely tourists

musing in Jackson
Square. The lamentable past
is better lost, and

the city does as
it has always done, slouching
towards oblivion

to withdraw among
the swamps where the long shadows
grow. We ride the dark

ferry alone, cold
in our cups and infinite
in mathematical

joy, the great diesels
driving us like a blunt plow
across the currents

and quick compulsions,
as unaware of the black
river as it is

of where it has been
or where in any lifetime
it will ever be.

The Truth You Heard

~

The truth you heard is wrong, is happy-hung
absurd inside your dumb and rusty heart,
love-sick and goat-jaw at the seams, wet tongue
of God a quick surprise of stop and start

and does-not-care, and if inside the breath
on which you fall asleep a prayer abides
within your chest, the crusty shibboleth
of violent ends, of trust in smallish lies,

perhaps you start to doubt the stumbled halls
of dreams that render in dissolve, in *mise
en scène* of box inside of box, so small
and so serene. So, then, the lie: a tree,

a sin, a careless whim, a flesh of rain,
and so the world, the loss, the lovely pain.

Sleeping Dogs Lie

⌒

Your dogs in their sleep
cat-roll in starts and whimpers,
their teeth snagged deep

in glories of fur
and slobbered skulls. No good
dog gives a good god

damn, and runs without
collar or care or you through
heavens of reeking

warm shit and bloody
mice newborn-wet in the fields.
When they wake,

they do not hope. Dreams
rot fragrantly wherever they've
fallen, shaken off

like rain and piss shivers.
Your dogs are all the sins you
leave yourself when

the wounds of childhood
subside. They have no hands to
borrow or bless you,

just dewclaws and spit
and wild noses to the crotch.
They grow old, they grow

indifferent as rags
full of must and carpet stains.
They do not love us

and they trust us just
so far. Their art is to love
themselves so wholly

that we become our
own spun gods, ablaze with self-
regard. No one knows

us always until
we die, and the dogwood rood
and driven nails are

no more blessed than
the purl and fetch of rancid
things, of meaningless

soft words and whistles,
of feces tender as damp
mushrooms in the grass.

Goethe's Apple

~

There is a housefly
humming, middle octave, key
of F, a frantic

agitata from
within the subtle skinned
bowl of the lightshade.

Erato, muse of
love, chews like a wasp larvae
through its ganglia

and yours alike, dark
smoked and raging. It wants
what it wandered here

to want, the thing its
sudden life so lacked it shags
its raisin body

rubato against
the veil of the temple, rent
not in twain

by the ghost given
up, but by the attar funk
of your sweat, perhaps,

or the brandy reek
of fruit fermenting softly
in the night kitchen.

Goethe, drunken, loathed
the barking of dogs, poodling
Mephistopheles

into *Faust* black as
necrosis, singing *trunken*
müssen wir alle

sein! to the little girls
in dirndls, aprons knotted
virgin-wise to the

front. But he adored
the smell of rotting apples,
and kept a single

sour *Glockenapfel*
growing vinegar and must
in the tippled first

drawer of his desk.
so that his words, fungal
and mephitic, twigged

across the pale pools
of foolscap like the subtle
blue veins of Lilith's

breasts, from clay formed
so as to tempt the winesap-
stained heart of rapture.

The man is become
like to one of us proclaimed
the lord from whose breath

are made the holy
orders, angels to scourge
the lost and evict

mad Faust from the pit
in which plump Gretchen languished,
pasty as knödel.

All theory is gray,
my friend, the devil mutters,
but forever green

is the tree of life,
and in the tree the apple
swings parlous and whole,

and from its virgin
pips subtle gardens grow to
breathe a sultry breeze

across the *liebchens'*
tender thighs, slick as an old
man's tongue, and in its

flesh a maggot waits,
a golden charm, a lover's
leer, a *mein engel*

lisped into an ear,
and at its core a razor's
blade, a gravity

of sleep to ride us
down into the gravid dirt
of our *schrecklich* hearts.

Three Quarks for Muster Mark

~

Three quarks for Muster Mark!
Sure he hasn't got much of a bark
And sure any he has it's all beside the mark.
—JAMES JOYCE, Finnigan's Wake

1.

Muster Mark drank his
quarks in some mucky Joyce-y
pub sprawled hard upon

the shit-foamed Liffey
where the seabirds choraled
overhoved and *shrill-*

gleescreaming and *yes*
was honey-meading between
the eggs and wordy

spoons. All you have to
do is look, and the world snaps
like a dry wishbone

into bird beaks and
rain pounding smackwarm, time just
one livid spry spark.

2.

What we were waits for
us somewhere like something a
tree has grown around,

a spar of old fence
or some kid's lost bicycle.
You can touch it, but

you can't take it, not
because it isn't yours any
more, but because it

isn't *you* any
more, the way your undressed bones
are yours but not *you,*

mouse bit and naked
in the anonymous dirt,
anonymously walked

upon by a foot
that shivers you crevice to
crown with *oh shit*, with

that gray-hour doubt
in the maker's calm making,
eigenstates kindly

superimposed with
loving intention so that
the fall when it comes

is only into
sinfulness and the simple
life with instructions:

the length of happy,
the breadth of moan grinding through
the night like loose teeth

and lucky little
straight-faced lies, like the one
about a way back

and no need to ask
how to get there or who gets
to stay out and play.

3.

A particle will
take absolutely every
possible path in

every possible
instant, nothing is left out,
nothing is wasted,

not even nothing,
because there is no such thing
as nothing. Plato

imagined the
chora, the quick space between
our being and our

becoming where all
possibility foams like
spittle into form

and formlessness, free
of intent and all regret
in the pea-soup sip

and suck of sea-change.
You imagine your children
as second comings,

as the world calling
you loving back from darkness
into soft raiment

and a storm of sweet
compulsions, new fields plowed
and ready for rain.

& you imagine
the word being said in the
darkness and the word

itself is darkness
and does not wait dog-simple
inside nothingness,

for a master's voice,
is not the face of the deep
nor the massless scream

of photons cracking
into the cheap-seat happy
of somehow being

& somehow being
seen. Is instead gulls and shit-
foamed river risen

into flood and growl,
is the voiceless knot of dream
addled seaswans sung

by the song, waters
floating a way a lone a
last, all the colors

of infinite and
infinitesimal a
born in between where

all spontaneous
does its strange leaving just for
us, just for us dies

its charmed becoming.

A Song on Geronimo's Grave

~

The sun, the darkness, the winds are listening . . .
—GERONIMO, Chief of the Bedonkohe Apache

1.

Boys, I shit you not,
it's Oklahoma, Billy
says, the Red River

more red than river
squatted under the border bridge
like the raw ass-end

of Mars, dry skin-peeled
under the flying rubber
of Billy's bald tires.

As I drive through the
valley of death, Billy says,
I will fear no fucked-

up Okies. I read
once, he says, that the Sanskrit
word for *war* means *we*

want more cows, just like
the word for *cows* in Okie
means *give us a kiss,*

cowboy. Of things
in Oklahoma worth one
single shit there are

only three, he says,
Geronimo's unstolen
bones, Oral Roberts

University
chromed like a starship, known to
every mother's son

in Tulsa as Six
Flags Over Jesus and fuck
if I can recall

the other one, and
as you rattle up from red
river mud to red

sooner dirt fighting
hard to blow away into
mischance and killing

grit, the casino
lights imagine themselves as
probabilities

and constellations
of uncertain compulsions
on the flayed horizon

and you say, *who's your
daddy, now?* and he says back,
who the bumfuck knows?

*Could be just about
anyone, or no mother-
lovin' one at all.*

2.

Watch me apache
my ass through the grass,
someone says, and goes

knees and elbows through
the stranded gravestones while you
imagine unborn

bees in six-sided
cells curled and wingless waiting
like dead Indians

still outraged and humming
in their boxes. You're twenty-
one, drunk and leaning

against the cobbled
stele over Geronimo's
grave, Oklahoma

summer midnight hot
behind your eyes and spinning
in its firmament.

You're singing something.
You can't remember the words,
even now. The past

is gone, peeled thin
and smeared on the back of your
eyelids like grease, black

with disappointment.
You're singing, and from somewhere
another voice sings,

all *sotto voce*
coy, along with you, wispy
cricket harmony

chanting deep in the
cochlear maze in your skull
where god speaks holy

to the prophets and
the young to tell them they are
naked and weak. It

has your name, the voice,
but it is not you. In all
the many worlds, when

one electron falls
nothing makes a sound, no spin
superpositions

with a soulless click,
spukhafte Fernwirkung, because
the particle becomes

you, entangles *you*
with the states of the system,
which is you, too, in

your drunk-spun glory,
snapped into the hardworn place
on a chief's tomb where

you churlish belong
and the voice, you-not-you, sings
the one note that is

the darkness without
judgment, breathlessly droning
inside your muscles

and nerves its soft *Om*
without cease, entangled with
all the raging dead.

The Law of the Excluded Middle

~

It is impossible, then, that 'being a man' should mean precisely
'not being a man.'   —ARISTOTLE, *Metaphysics*

Together comes down
every time to someone to
complain about or

someone to complain
to. Lesson learned, fault taken,
separate kept, as

always, separate.
And still, O lord, the longing
for the sublime and

single *other* who
can make it past, set it right,
bring us home again.

Shelley, drowned poet,
was buried where he was found,
and ten days on they

lugged, his oldest friends,
a cast iron furnace down to
the sea and wedged him

crab-picked in, smothered
like a plaice in gardenias,
wine and olive oil.

His black poet's eyes
crawled like snails when the fire
split his skull. To Mary,

they brought his blackened
heart, wrapped in a poem so dark
it drew blood and pale

beads of marrow from
the air like dew. Life went on.
Around his absence

leaves and poppies grew.
And still it was just one heart
tirelessly crooning

its losses. She grew
old, stood nude before the seas
of winter, between

rusting sky and wind.
She made of him a looking
glass, reprise of ash,

of poet's hands and
crab-picked skin, a shared breath to
never breathe again.

Hard Pearl

~

... he entertained that the souls of the dead are enclosed in the bean.
—PLINY THE ELDER, *Historia Natural*

No farther out than this apostate star
unclenching in the wimpled dusk, the tense
burlesque of *In the beginning* begins to stir.
New marble dies and goes rigid against

a chisel like old love, and spiral skeins
of gas collapse and scrum into the light
of souls compressed to fit inside of beans,
the misplaced dead that Pliny thought survived

so as to make their way through each of us
like quantum particles arising back
into the world that is and never was,
becoming lime-hard grains of distilled black

to pearl our hollows with refining fire,
the stony ache of absence and desire.

The Lesser Poet

~

You plant rocks to grow
nothing, and, like Sylvia,
patron saint of not

a bloody thing, never
wash any part of you save
your fingertips where

the touch of holy
blessing burns you clean of sin
and aspiration.

No one kills the poets
because no one really has
to, except when they

do, a smattering,
Stalin's baker's dozen
shot all together

like a choir, the
occasional Somali
or Chechen murdered

for mattering. You
long to not belong, you long
for secret things and

mirrors full of breath
and brevity and the names
of artifice scrawled

backwards like muses
bruising your misanthropic
heart with cold kisses

and sharp-filed fairy
teeth. The consonant mantra
of to-be-empty-

is-to-be-full pulls
coptic at your nerves. Tremble,
lesser poet, sack

of winds! The moon skids
icy into daylit bloom
and there you hard-nailed

hang, marooned in a
a wasted life in which you
never died too young.

And Yet It Moves

~

Who can say we know all there is to know?
—GALILEO GALILEI, *Letter to Castelli*

Eppur si muove
Galileo pointedly
whispered, or perhaps

didn't, the Roman
Inquisition watching his
hunched heretical

back tottering out
the door. Better to ask *what
ever stands still in*

this immovable
life? God's little joke
go boom, squirrel-cage

hyperactive, wild
spun through the veritable
sky, endless as pi.

His abjuration
made, Galileo homeward
went, to cows and cats

and utter blindness,
stars dusting the chary lens
of his inner eye.

Easier to be
stopped than to stop, duck-
ugly in the pond

of universal
wrong but by-god still swimming,
still chin above the

swill. *Knowing* never
is enough; better to *be*
known in the hog-slop

sanity of three-
formed Saturn floated gravy
and meat in his bowl,

cats fish-fat sleepy
in his lap, while the darkness
spins its lovely lies.

Playful Song Called Beautiful

~

This playful song called beautiful, listen if you will.
—Blurb on an album of Chinese Children's Songs

Do not use pool while
fiery rain. The grass is smiles
at you, do please

not disturb, tiny
grass is dreaming like precious
picture, you naïve

smiling face. Sorry,
the machine was out of truth.
Today is under

construction, thanks you
for waiting. Bitter row of
children in each small

package. There's a wrong
coupling frown in every one.
Welcome to here, it

is space you can find
many breads. Open them here,
all of them are you.

The Lost Children

~

A seagull stole him from his slow mama's hands.
—ENGRISH BWUDD, "Man Man"

Dingo-baby gone,
wandered off, scooped up, fumbled
windward in mighty

chords, the lost children
for love or thrills or hunger
meddle in baffling

absentia. They know
nothing and care less. When you
nail your life closed, they

find some peeled corner
and crawl inside like nibbling
mice to make trashy

nests and chew your bones
into whistles and pitchy
flutes. Like cats, they don't

go where they're wanted,
which is the white-washed Limbo
of nowhere at all.

They never wronged
anyone, so now they wrong
everyone, subtle

guilts and kinks, lusts you
never wanted, bad seeds hot
sprouting like fungi

and disappointment
in your nether voids and fear-
clenched spaces to itch

and fester where life
meets death, coming and going
with each token breath.

The Thing Itself Speaks

~

Even the evening
denies itself, tangled
angry and confused

on the brushy red
horizon like some kid caught
cookie-handed on

his way out the door.
Always something explaining
its unfaithful heart

away, all shaman
and brassy-cool *res ipsa
loquitur,* moments

before the locks shank closed.
Don't bother, you want to tell
the light, as if it

were someone who could
listen, there are other things
to love us, abstract

and damned near as chill.
The trees scratching nails across
the dusk's bloody

ass stand aching and
self-evident as sin, stripped
to a finer shade

of winter bleak, in
cold hues of stubborn. Wind would
be too much, so there

isn't any, even,
to die away as the thing
itself drops *bête noire*

among us like some ghost
we don't believe in until
we do, this *other*

we've never seen, so
thin you can breathe it in like
the oddly lovely

stink of compromise.
It's why the older we get,
the more we linger

within, where the walls
mute the diesel-horn howling
that shivers us stem

to rotten stern in
our flotsam and riches, as
we rub our *amor*

fati hopes like charms
for luck. *I want to see as*
beautiful all that

is necessary,
Nietzsche said, but the beauty
squeals out the cracks

like the huffing hot
breath of your furnace and the
necessary hangs

ugly in every
whistling eave where we feed it
and watch it grow, black

as mold, into the thing
becoming itself as we
resigned, become ours.

What We Want

~

We want twenty amps
straight to the heart. We want to
suck someone else's

nerves like five wicked
flavors of new. What our gods
didn't make of us

we by god make of
ourselves, out of whatever
cauls and baby toothed

dissatisfactions
are left over when the fire's
out and the wailing's

begun. We behave
badly, brother. We fling shit
and sulk luck-busted

in our juices, and when
the wind blows our little house
down we build it up

again, and fuck us
for even *trying* to have
something nice, something

to love and squander
when every little blessed
thing is ours to lose.

What we want, *O what*
we want, is for one breath to
follow another

forever, wheezing
towards a cosmological
singularity

in which we alone
diverge to infinity
and become our own lonely

god from whose lucent
breath meaningless static roars
into gravity

and light and the three
blind forms of desire, still
us, still meaningless

as the music one-
toned from which the frenetic
complexity of

hearts and stars erupts
into the anguish that's all
we ever wanted.

Quod Me Nutrit Me Destruit

～

As for myself, I walk abroad a-nights,
And kill sick people groaning under walls.
—CHRISTOPHER MARLOWE, *The Jew of Malta*

1.

Imagine the way
the iron prodded vicious through
the cracker thin bone-

back of his eye with
a sound like a bad tooth giving
way, Marlowe board stiff,

still standing, sclera
and iris split into wet
staring hemispheres,

and then local time-
asymmetry, such as it
was, took over, and

the raw entropy
of his fall to the dirt floor
connected spark-bright

to the expansion
of the known universe at
its earliest evolution

in one hot screaming
bodhisattva breath holy
as infinity.

2.

Water drops skitter
in a hot skillet, flicked
from the five gracile

aspergillum of
her finger tips. Oil next, then
the egg, following

the apocryphal
arrow of time from ovum's
untethered order

to omelet. On her
wrist tattooed Latin: *Quod Me
Nutrit Me Destruit*,

motto of murdered
playwrights and anorexics
and fine descriptor

of the deep nature
of *thusness*, though she does not
care if creation's

open veins drain white
the eleven kinds of suns
or if the coffee

in its porcelain
tasse takes the milk she pours
in slow turning gyres

and makes of it the
cloudless secret perfection
of pure disorder.

3.

The luminous pick
descending into Trotsky's
skull—a line from a

poem floating white-rag
in the foamy suck and tide
of your mind. Nothing

is easy in this shit-
happens life. Borges claimed
that the infinite

is the one complete
evil corrupting all, but
all the incomplete

evils somehow seem
infinite enough. We long
for souls to go like

Indian scouts on
ahead into the fiction
of ever-after

and tell us what we
mean, but instead we get poets
and philosophers,

those wet bags of bad
news. Trotsky humped over
his desk is reading

and around his head
the cosmos turns in all the
possible postures

of revolution,
no fate quite yet sealed. He
is thinking, maybe,

of speaking, the first
word forming like a single
probability

on the crisp blue
edge of collapse, a hand,
not his, reaching for

the wooden handle
of a kind of love. Outside
his open window

the laurel trees on
the Avendia Río
Churubusco point

relentlessly out
to the end of everything
forty-five billion

dust-smeared light-years
away, where the *surface of
last scattering* lies

in the decoupled
photon hiss of genesis
and as the ice pick

begins its soundless
arc each tree shivers inside
the lost germ of new

potential from which
it grew, singing like temple
bells rung in the first

gray light of pity.

Evil Pockets

~

Promises were made,
my friend, and promises were
damned well broken.

Geryon, son of
Chrysaor and Callirrhoe,
grandson of gorgons,

dwelt large and wine born
in the damp Hesperides,
and then a setback

or two, some bad calls
and shitty breaks and next thing
he's playing taxi

for poets around
the tenfold evil pockets
of *Malebolge*, all

jolly-faced and
scorpion-assed so Dante
could stare down at all

the faces staring
up at the lucky bastards
circling their dry rings

of lesser pain, down
to where evil itself stands
locked in frozen tears,

jaws full of the hot
lying meats of Judas
and Brutus and lean

Cassius who thought
too much and so was pitched
like a bloody rag

into this bone-chill
cervix of lostness. There is
no deeper *in it*

into which you can
get than that, rolled like gristle
'tween Satan's rotten

gums, though of course that's
not how it feels, lying dead-
turtle on your back

on a gurney, skull
slamming nitroglycerin
fists in a clever

panic as the pill
sublingual dissolves and you
think you hear a juke

box playing a song
somewhere, some bleety number,
and you realize

you haven't grasped
until this moment that it's
anticipation,

all of it, promise
and fulfillment, every erg
of wasted effort

you've lived resolves to
if this, then that, plant seed, reap
seed, little demons

of consistency,
the *Malebranche* claw-hooked
inside your throbbing

glands and threads like hands
in evil pockets, *evil*
in the first Sanskrit

sense of *gone too far,*
so many plump carcasses
bloating in ditches

among the blackberry
vines and sunlit grass, all the
hollow places left

behind, whisper-shaped
and snug as coffins. The space
you fill is who you

are and who you are
is nothing. No pit, nor fire,
nor vinegared ash

to feed the lambs poured
like lead into molds of clay
that leak them away

in worms and marrows.
You are hands tucked inside some
hebetic pocket

of waiting until
someone pulls you free and you
open as hands will

do, filled with only
your first last breath as you bow
your throbbing head and

breathe it deeply in.

Desirada

~

. . . it is still a beautiful world. / Be careful.   —MAX EHRMAN

Go placidly from
the wet paper bag of sleep,
from the fisted black

river pebbles dry-
scrape in their orbits, the six
different ways you

say *I am me* when
the visions and night portents
shake you crumb and soul

out of the sheets. Do
not want what you don't deserve
or dip your fingers

in the styx-softened
blood of martyrs and frauds. Do
not, for god's simple

sake, trust anyone.
There are heroes about, but
they do not know you,

and the universe,
for what it's worth, minds its own
damned business. Every

breath you breathe was spit
and steam in some sun's straining
bowel, and that taste

on your tongue is blood
and frightful indifference.
Live, if you can, with

knowing that evil
drifts in the air like pollen,
like skin mandolined

into dust by a
fingernail eased along
the pale shaven arc

of a stranger's *mons*.
It is still a terrible
world, friend. Be grateful.

The Ghosts of Birds

~

They never quite alight on these bare nests
of rat-chewed shells and bones they haunt. They come
and go from crowded lines in vagrant wisps
of cat and nerve and endless horsefly hum

above the patient evening streets gone black
with flesh crushed thin as every last regret.
Their hollow bones leak zippered trails of smoke
across a brutal neon sky, and yet

they linger, Holy Ghost and salted tails,
in children's nameless dreams of God's intent
to make his bread and angels of their pale
and smallish souls spun through his firmament

and back again like ghosts of birds that fly
as feathered light inside their sleeping eyes.

Why You Leave

~

The wind erodes your will to stay like spume
on sand, slams so appalling many doors
berserker shut like teeth and so goddamn
just-like-that, chainsaw-fast until the air

is raw with closing, with all you've alleged
to love reduced road-kill into the many
unspoken names of any mortal god
a man may whisper *sotto voce* in

the dark for luck. Inside the kept color
of lavish is the dark itself, bebopping
like breath against your mind, a dull dolor
of what-the-hell that just won't bloody stop

until your drums of joy and bone go still
and wind and careless world have had their fill.

If I Should Die Before I Wake

~

If you do not die young you do not live,
at least not well—you know too much to give

a good goddamn, and when a door appears
upon a perfect bending arc that soars

above the breathless grace of gravity
you topple through and all the brevity

of your falling falls with you, ash and stem
and wailing light that crawls the honeyed limbs

of lying trees in which a question swings
like bats or children waiting in the wings

to ride the febrile currents of their blood
into each tender morning shaped in mud

and sprinkled with fine sugar sand as white
as any ghost surrendered in the night.

The Gift

~

You hold your tongue your
mother said, and so you did,
twofingered like some

grotty thing no one
should touch, dead-pigeon maggot-
quivering when she

slapped you hard then cried,
the both of you. You still want
to gift her something

irredeemable
so it can't be gifted back,
some gloried violent

gaud like the freckled
copy of de Sade's *Justine
et Juliette* bound

in tanned human skin
taken from the cadaver
breasts of a dead girl

you saw in a cave
of a *librairie* in the
Faubourg Saint-Germain,

or better yet a clean
unraveled skein of painless
nights and lucid days,

bound in the compound
humors of green leaves and sure
things like a poultice

against forgetting,
against wickedness, against
the tithe of regret

we gift to ourselves.

What Happens When You Stop

~

The map of your sewn life opens then like
a fungus bursting, flowers open, and
in that life there are no corners, no flakes
of godly skin, no roads, and every dead

or dying end is home where light leaks out
each frameless door you've never walked into.
Open was never hard. You should not doubt
out loud, you shouldn't have unpacked, or screwed

yourself tick-tight into this life of day
too late and night too short because you want
these things you want, and that's the wrong you pray
to right by stopping here, some dilettante

the sun shines blind, until the stitches tear
on all the light an unsewn mind can bear.

What is Left

~

Inevitably,
is the bottom-scrape and back-
wash, soft fruit to keep

you company, old
bones and early morning ink
black like ashes thumbed

across your forehead,
like an X on a mall map
to show you that you

are, for the moment,
here, between the sentence and
the light, where gardens

grow in the ripe-shift
molder of your mind and all
the *yous* you've suffered

and loved chew fat-rat
through your tender meat until
all that's left is you.

Dog Dreams

~

When you're dead and your
dogs howl coyote, twitchy
with dreams of rapine

and wander, smelling
your puddling cells in their sleep
and longing doggy

style to roll feet up
in the liquid stink of you,
when you, fool that you

are, break like bread, like
gristle in a grinder, beasts
will sip the organ-y

blow and gag of your
countable breaths and tongue-cup
your last hoary smile

like marrow, a psalm
they sing to you so that you,
dead, can sing it, too.

Mésalliance Grotesque

～

The seventeen folds of *orizuru*.
The hymns before amens. The things that love
you and wherein that love abides. So blue

these sacramental anatomies, rough
as some windfallen peach, a stone inside
a withered fist, but gently, gently, stuff

of spells and divination bones to hide
how little you deserve the smallest gift
that gives itself to you. The winter tide

of chastity. The one vow left to sift
with stars and chains, with comets flung around
in rings through voids of happiness. You drift

inside this lie, that worlds eternal sound
unchanging crystal spheres of aether, spun
like aggies inside goblets, round and round.

The *natural place* toward which all bodies wane
is just a lie, and the *unmoved mover*
is just a lie bedamned and water-stained,

abandoned in a ditch. You fall a blur
of leaf-sway through the sky where what loves you
just might endure as maps of fallen stars

to show the sullen vines of longing through
which bony trellis they might grow because
you always let them and they always do,

to fill the space where wings once sung in you.

Turing Lies with Men

~

Turing believes machines think,
Turing lies with men,
Therefore machines do not think.
> —ALAN TURING, in a letter to Norman Routledge, 1952

Turing lies with men,
and God rages from the hills,
mad with piety,

tattooed Māori-blunt
with the scatty *ta moko*
ashes of the razed

cities of the plain.
Turing lies with men, and brown-
shirted children give

him poisoned apples
and cannibal teeth. Sex, like
inquest, is a kind

of calculation,
cryptic and as veritable
as one and zero.

A machine would know
this, would hold the single thought
like a lover's breath

floated in the dark,
faithless first premise of a
promise: Turing lies

with men, and within
the enigmas of ardor,
men with Turing lie,

tucked in the oiled thrum-
thrust of their fell paradise
under a sky smeared

with ruin and secrets
like tongues grazing the edges
of his wanton mind.

Turing lies with men,
and the gazing world sizzles
in the white static

of its compulsions,
immaculate with self-love
and pale equations.

Blood Rain at Stoke Edith

~

There was a bloody rain in Britain. And milk and butter were turned
to blood.   —*The Anglo-Saxon Chronicle*

You walk hand in hand
and wish for blood or butter
or both. Stoke Edith

is tongue-in-the-ear
quaint, all English village rain
and tea-cozy stodge

curdling in corners,
some kids pretending to be
corruption and smoke

under the lipped eave
of a pub. There is only
so far you can go

until you're here, so
many people you can be
until you're not. The

rain is just rain, cold
and ordinary country-
holy, colorless

windflick spittle, not
gore pissing rudely upon
the pavements. Mary

Godsall saw Christ's blood
fall here *upon Wednesday*
the 16 instant

July, the year
1769, and felt
it splatter-shot red

onto her cow's flank,
into the milk gone murky
pink in her bucket,

into her eyes and
her mouth wide-O to the sky's
running wounds, tasting

of salt-fish and frog-
spawn, blood turned to wine and no
priest to turn it back

again, and *gods, what*
terror! pooling on her tongue,
like slow starvation

or learning to forgive
a savior who chose of all
people you to bear

this vision that stains
even now the sky above
Stoke Edith milky

coral, the clouds shot
through with old scars like contrails,
and the hand in your

hand is blood-wimpled
and wet and you are drowning
slowly in the way

they say farmed turkeys
do back in the states, staring
up at something not

quite there, a steady rain
of blessings falling where you
have no right to be.

Here Where We Are Terrible

~

We polish ourselves
to a shine, grinding circles
in the invert palms

of our hands like flies
working dogshit into its
simplest settled self,

the pellicular
glister of our self-regard
become a scalar

quality of time
without direction or sense,
the rumble of hot

ticking like a rage
of snare-drummy bluesy-ness
beating out the light.

All day long we get
it wrong, crazed with fiberglass
itch, trying to rub

through skin and sloppy
skeins of veins to the bundles
of brittle we're made

from, rattle and rust
and sunny windrows of frost
edging the tire-cut

mud of Florida
backroad winter where the eye
ends on rough-cut seas

and mangrove clutter
in the cold mismatched distance
of lost perspective

and what we've given
and forgiven eddies out
of the salt-hazed blur

of far horizons
like yellow marrow and on
it, floated farthest

out of all, is one
lousy lost boat pinned donkey
tail blind on what might

be the water, what
might be the sky, what in fact
might be the slow dry

run of what we were
afraid to find, finding us,
terrible ones, who

imagine a tight
skitter of desperate code
out there, Save Our Souls

tossed across the waves
straight to us and only us
to crackle candy-

wrapper loud inside
our skulls with the wondrous news
of someone else's

suffering, out there
where we are not the worst thing
that can happen but

the best, and god's own
answer to the taciturn
stars that watch and wait,

but here, we tell them,
is where we are terrible,
where we turn our backs

and go home, too far
gone to care about a hole
still finger-tapping

its lapsing boat-ness
at the birds that come on wing
to mark our absence.

The Things You Can't Keep

~

Werner Heisenberg's
gravestone predicts *He Lies Here,*
Somewhere with the kind

of confidence stones
tend to pretend, making hay,
like history, with

us or without us.
The lies are ours, but little
more. We can't keep bent

clavicles like wings,
or seraphim like bats hung
pug-faced in the dim

belfries where the old
names that know us cross themselves
and chitter. We can't

keep the burnt-hair reek
of witch fires or the change gone
verdigris in our

pockets and swear jars,
or even the pauses when
our pictures are snapped

in which we smile, charmed
at the margins if not in
the meat. What we can't

keep peels from the curled
backs of photographs like school
paste, crawls worm-love through

our every soft part
and fancy, throbs bone-ugly
in our click-clack hands,

in the mud and wet
bloom that loaned us our first fey
ghosts as the mountains

broke the light like bread
over our mornings, that we might
take but never have.

We miss the silver
pearl of breath squeezed from the space
between our breastbones

and our backbones like
the ice-cracked stone in the stream,
except there is no

stone, only stream cut
with crushing glades of sunglare
and flux under which

a branch flicks a lone
finger, endlessly annoyed
like an aunt tapping

your empty skull with   .
a thimble to remind you
of the grim burdens

you were born to, like
the kittens birthed yesterday
beneath the kitchen

floor, each complaining
in the doubled dark about
its bewildering

consciousness, the milk
and mouse stink, the hard-dried scab
of parting puckered

on its belly, first
things gone in sudden breathless
hush, tumbled eighty

miles to the cold gulf
where gulls wait at the aching
edge of everything

to pick through burlap
and bone scrap for the nameless
things that no one kept.

Shooting Dove

⌒

Watch your lead, he says,
catch it on the rise. Sweep on
past and take it when

the muzzle grazes
the beak. Watch for the climbers
over the trees, they're

the ones, streaking-rare,
impossibly manifest, that sweep
the glistered sunlight

through the cedar elms
and strip the breath from your lungs
like something you can't

afford to lose, and
as you raise the stock to your
face, weight on your back

foot, the bird palled
by the muzzle's sudden void,
a child will fall clean

from the half-held bowl
of sky, torn with yearning, through
your one open eye.

Iowa Poetry Prize and Edwin Ford Piper
Poetry Award Winners

～

1987   Elton Glaser, *Tropical Depressions*
       Michael Pettit, *Cardinal Points*

1988   Bill Knott, *Outremer*
       Mary Ruefle, *The Adamant*

1989   Conrad Hilberry, *Sorting the Smoke*
       Terese Svoboda, *Laughing Africa*

1990   Philip Dacey, *Night Shift at the Crucifix Factory*
       Lynda Hull, *Star Ledger*

1991   Greg Pape, *Sunflower Facing the Sun*
       Walter Pavlich, *Running near the End of the World*

1992   Lola Haskins, *Hunger*
       Katherine Soniat, *A Shared Life*

1993   Tom Andrews, *The Hemophiliac's Motorcycle*
       Michael Heffernan, *Love's Answer*
       John Wood, *In Primary Light*

1994   James McKean, *Tree of Heaven*
       Bin Ramke, *Massacre of the Innocents*
       Ed Roberson, *Voices Cast Out to Talk Us In*

1995   Ralph Burns, *Swamp Candles*
       Maureen Seaton, *Furious Cooking*

1996   Pamela Alexander, *Inland*
Gary Gildner, *The Bunker in the Parsley Fields*
John Wood, *The Gates of the Elect Kingdom*

1997   Brendan Galvin, *Hotel Malabar*
Leslie Ullman, *Slow Work through Sand*

1998   Kathleen Peirce, *The Oval Hour*
Bin Ramke, *Wake*
Cole Swensen, *Try*

1999   Larissa Szporluk, *Isolato*
Liz Waldner, *A Point Is That Which Has No Part*

2000   Mary Leader, *The Penultimate Suitor*

2001   Joanna Goodman, *Trace of One*
Karen Volkman, *Spar*

2002   Lesle Lewis, *Small Boat*
Peter Jay Shippy, *Thieves' Latin*

2003   Michele Glazer, *Aggregate of Disturbances*
Dainis Hazners, *(some of) The Adventures of Carlyle,
My Imaginary Friend*

2004   Megan Johnson, *The Waiting*
Susan Wheeler, *Ledger*

2005   Emily Rosko, *Raw Goods Inventory*
        Joshua Marie Wilkinson, *Lug Your Careless Body out
        of the Careful Dusk*

2006   Elizabeth Hughey, *Sunday Houses the Sunday House*
        Sarah Vap, *American Spikenard*

2008   Andrew Michael Roberts, *something has to happen next*
        Zach Savich, *Full Catastrophe Living*

2009   Samuel Amadon, *Like a Sea*
        Molly Brodak, *A Little Middle of the Night*

2010   Julie Hanson, *Unbeknownst*
        L. S. Klatt, *Cloud of Ink*

2011   Joseph Campana, *Natural Selections*
        Kerri Webster, *Grand & Arsenal*

2012   Stephanie Pippin, *The Messenger*

2013   Eric Linsker, *La Far*
        Alexandria Peary, *Control Bird Alt Delete*

2014   JoEllen Kwiatek, *Study for Necessity*

2015   John Blair, *Playful Song Called Beautiful*
        Lindsay Tigue, *System of Ghosts*